Flags World

Liberia
Libya
Lithuania
Luxembourg
Macedonia, FYRO
Madagascar
Malawi
Malaysia
Maldives
Mali
Malta
Mauritania
Mexico
Moldova
Monaco
Mongolia
Montenegro
Morocco
Mozambique
Myanmar
Namibia
Nepal
Netherlands
New Zealand
Nicaragua
Niger
Nigeria
North Korea
Norway
Oman
Pakistan
Panama
Papua New Guinea
Paraguay
Peru
Philippines
Poland
Portugal
Qatar
Romania
Russia
Rwanda
St. Lucia
Saudi Arabia
Senegal
Serbia
Sierra Leone
Singapore
Slovakia
Slovenia
Somalia
South Africa
South Korea
Spain
Sri Lanka
Sudan
Sweden
Switzerland
Syria
Taiwan
Tanzania
Thailand
Trinidad and Tobago
Tunisia
Turkey
Turkmenistan
Uganda
Ukraine
United Arab Emirates
United Kingdom
United States of America
Uruguay
Uzbekistan
Venezuela
Vietnam
Yemen
Zambia
Zimbabwe

Oxford Very First Atlas

Editorial Adviser
Dr Patrick Wiegand

OXFORD
UNIVERSITY PRESS

Great Clarendon Street, Oxford OX2 6DP

Oxford University Press is a department of the University of Oxford.
It furthers the University's objective of excellence in research, scholarship,
and education by publishing worldwide in

Oxford   New York

Auckland Cape Town Dar es Salaam Hong Kong Karachi
Kuala Lumpur Madrid Melbourne Mexico City Nairobi
New Delhi Shanghai Taipei Toronto

With offices in

Argentina Austria Brazil Chile Czech Republic France Greece
Guatemala Hungary Italy Japan Poland Portugal Singapore
South Korea Switzerland Thailand Turkey Ukraine Vietnam

Oxford is a registered trade mark of Oxford University Press
in the UK and in certain other countries

ISBN 978 0 19 848787 6 (hardback)
ISBN 978 0 19 848786 9 (paperback)

1 3 5 7 9 10 8 6 4 2

Printed in Singapore by KHL Printing Co. Pte Ltd.

Paper used in the production of this book is a natural, recyclable product
made from wood grown in sustainable forests. The manufacturing process
conforms to the environmental regulations of the country of origin.

TEACHERS
For inspirational support plus
free resources and eBooks
www.oxfordprimary.co.uk

PARENTS
Help your child's reading
with essential tips, fun
activities and free eBooks
www.oxfordowl.co.uk

Acknowledgements

The publishers would like to thank Roderick Hunt for his advice on literacy levels.

The publishers would like to thank the following for permission to reproduce photographs:

Alamy pp 13 (Roger Cracknell), 22 (Visions of America, LLC), 23 (Gary Cook), 25 (Dave Watts),
26 (PeterArnold Inc.), 27 (Steven J. Kazlowski), 29 (John Macpherson); Photolibrary Group pp7 (Radius Images),
21 (Jochen Tack), 32 (Brian Lawrence); Science Photo Library pp 5 (Planetary Visions Ltd), 6 (Planetary Visions
Ltd), 8t (Planetary Visions Ltd), 8b (Planetobserver), 10-11 (Planetobserver), 28 (Planetobserver).
All other photographs supplied by Oxford University Press.

Cover illustrations by Galia Bernstein. Cover globe by Jan Rysavy/iStockphoto.

Contents

Greetings from
THE ALPS

Having fun in
PARIS

On holiday in
INDIA

A postcard from
NEW YORK

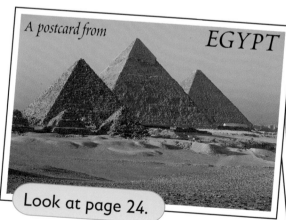

A postcard from
EGYPT

Greetings from
LONDON

Can you find these places in the atlas?

Planet Earth

World maps

Continents and oceans

The British Isles

4　This is space.

The Earth is a planet in space.

6 The Earth is round, like a ball.

Satellites take pictures of the Earth.

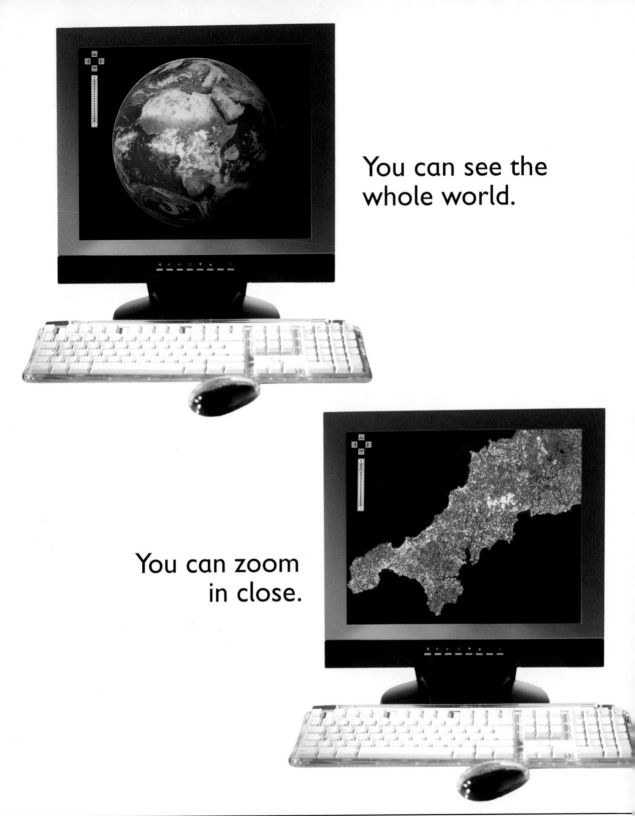

You can see the whole world.

You can zoom in close.

These are satellite pictures on a computer.

The Earth has
land and sea.

A globe is a model of the Earth.

The World

10   This is a picture of the Earth from space.

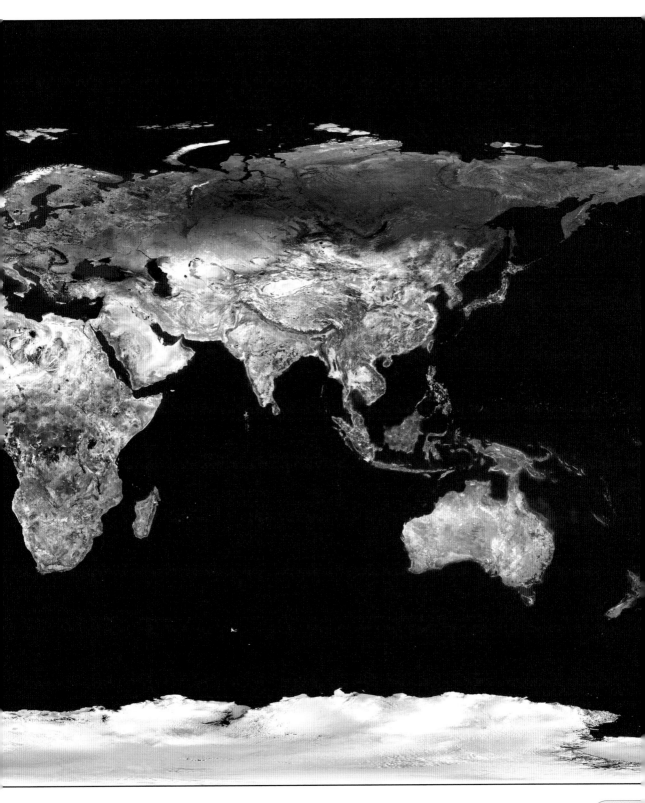

It is laid out flat.

The World

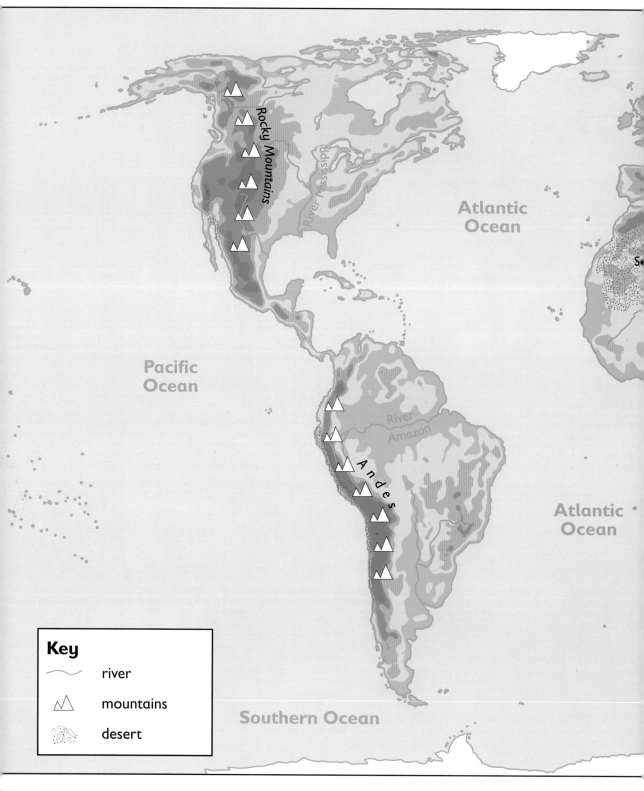

Rocky Mountains

River Mississippi

Atlantic Ocean

Pacific Ocean

River Amazon

Andes

Atlantic Ocean

Southern Ocean

Key

∼	river
⋀	mountains
⛰	desert

This is a map of the world.

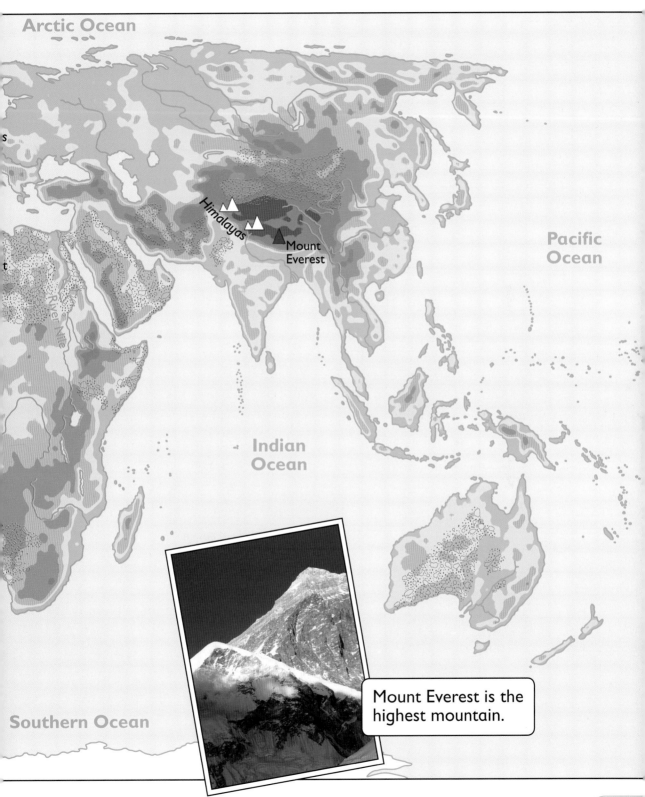

Arctic Ocean

Pacific
Ocean

Himalayas

Mount
Everest

River Nile

Indian
Ocean

Mount Everest is the
highest mountain.

Southern Ocean

It shows rivers, mountains and deserts.

The World

North America

South America

This is a map of Antarctica.

Antarctica

⌐South Pole

The world has seven continents.

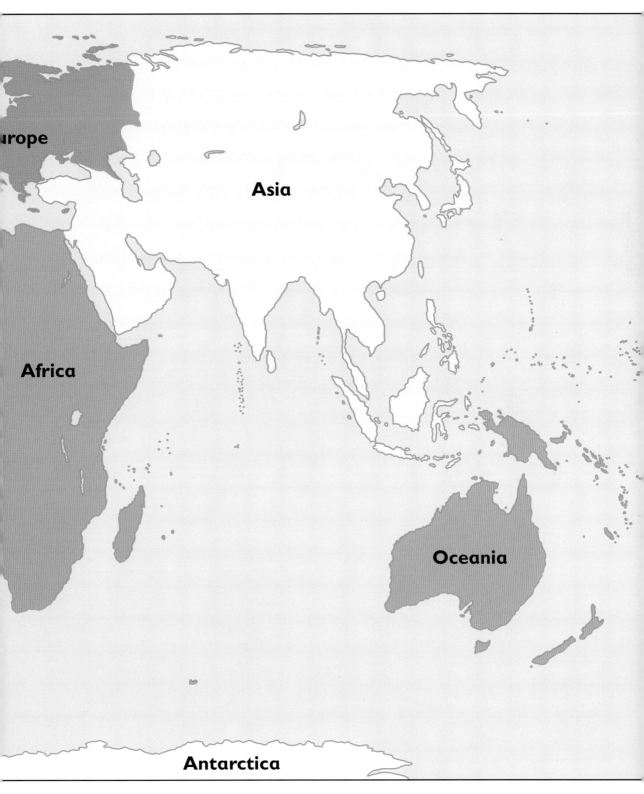

urope

Asia

Africa

Oceania

Antarctica

Continents are very big areas of land.

The World

Canada

United Kingdom

United States of America

F

S

Morocco

N

Mexico

Colombia

Brazil

Peru

Bolivia

Chile

Argentina

Key

Colours show countries.

The world has many countries.

Russia

Japan

China

Iran

Pakistan

ɔya

Egypt

Saudi Arabia

India

Philippines

had

Sudan

Ethiopia

Kenya

Tanzania

Indonesia

ngola

Madagascar

Australia

South Africa

New Zealand

Which country are you from?

Europe

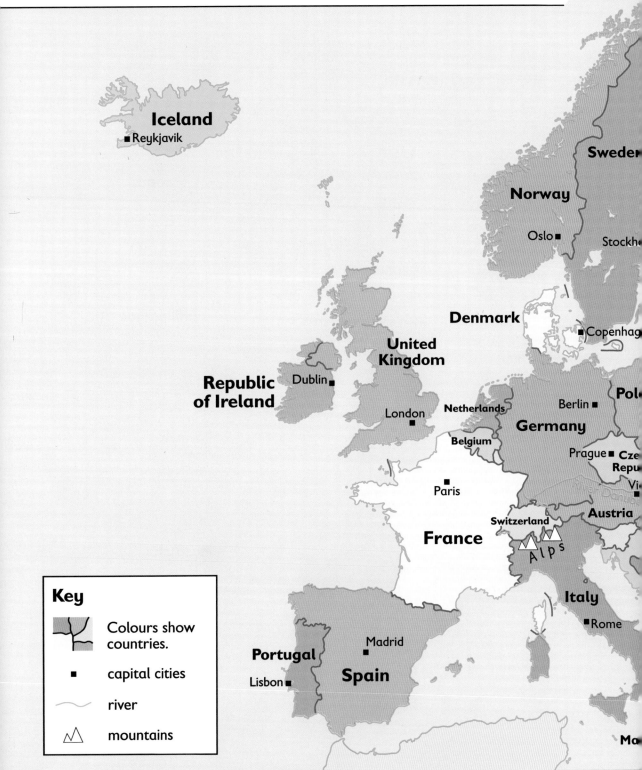

Iceland
- Reykjavik

Norway
Oslo ■

Sweden

Stockh

Denmark
■ Copenhag

United
Kingdom

Republic
of Ireland

Dublin ■

London ■

Netherlands

Belgium

Berlin ■

Germany

Prague ■ Cze
Repu

Pol

Vie
■

Austria

Paris ■

Switzerland

Alps

Italy

France

Rome ■

Madrid ■

Portugal

Lisbon ■

Spain

Ma

Key

Colours show countries.

■   capital cities

~   river

⋀   mountains

Europe is a small continent.

Finland

Helsinki

Tallinn
Estonia

Riga
Latvia

thuania
Vilnius

Minsk

Belarus

aw

Kiev

Ukraine

Russia

Moscow

River Volga

Romania

grade Bucharest

a

Bulgaria

Sofia

eece

Athens

Georgia
Tbilisi

Ankara

Turkey

Cyprus

Hello   Hola   Buon giorno

God dag   Guten Tag

Bonjour   Yia sas

Dzień dobry   Merhaba

There are many European languages.

Asia

Asia is the largest continent.

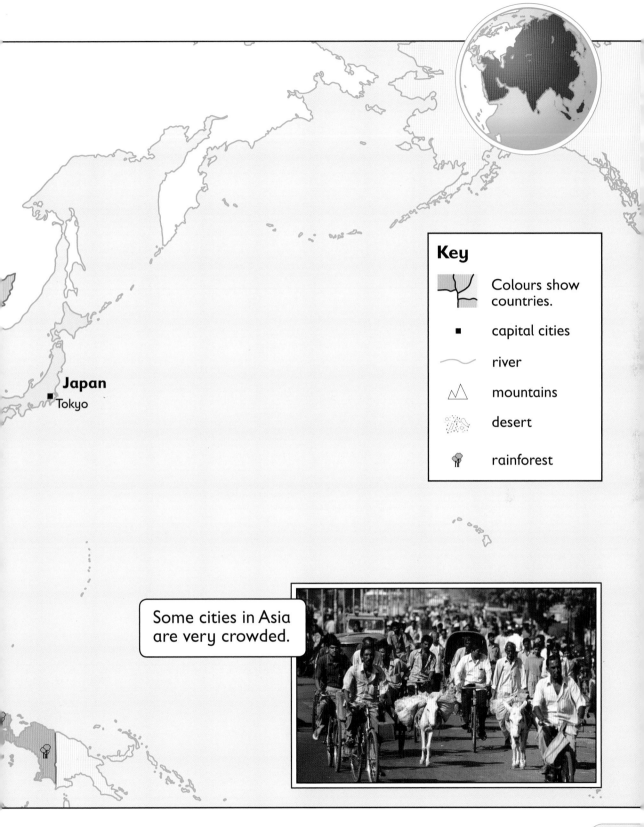

Japan
■ Tokyo

Key

	Colours show countries.
■	capital cities
~	river
△	mountains
	desert
🌳	rainforest

Some cities in Asia are very crowded.

It also has the most people.

North America

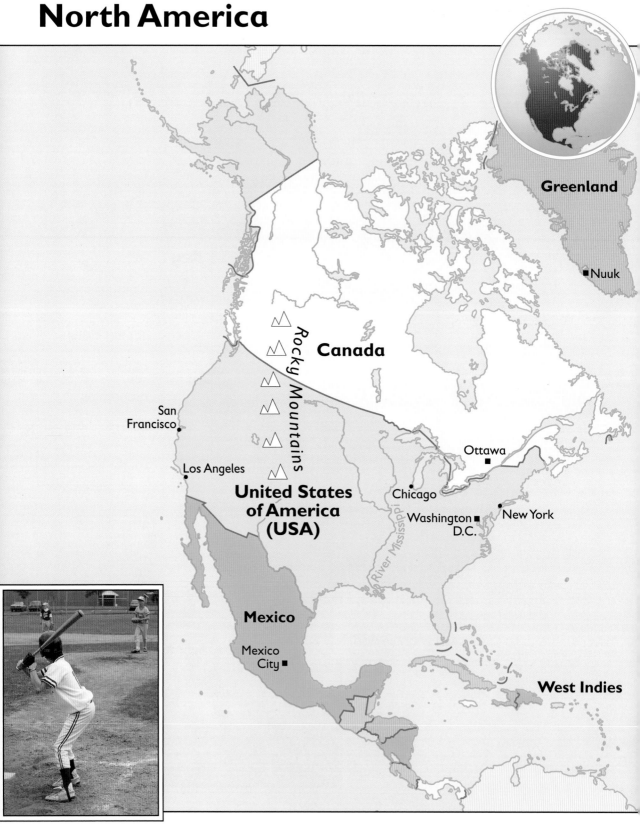

Greenland

■ Nuuk

Rocky Mountains

Canada

San Francisco

Los Angeles

United States of America (USA)

Ottawa ■

Chicago

Washington ■ New York
D.C.

River Mississippi

Mexico

Mexico City ■

West Indies

The USA is the world's richest country.

South America

Caracas

Venezuela

Georgetown

Paramaribo
Cayenne

Bogota

Colombia

Guyana

Suriname

French Guiana

Quito
Ecuador

River Amazon

A
n
d
e
s

B r a z i l

Lima

Peru

Bolivia

La Paz

Brasilia

A
n
d
e
s

Paraguay

Asuncion

C
h
i
l
e

Argentina

Santiago

Uruguay

Buenos Aires

Montevideo

A
n
d
e
s

Key

Colours show
countries.

- ■ capital cities
- • other cities
- ~ river
- ⋀⋀ mountains
- 🌳 rainforest

It rains a lot in the
Amazon rainforest.

There is a big rainforest in Brazil.

Africa

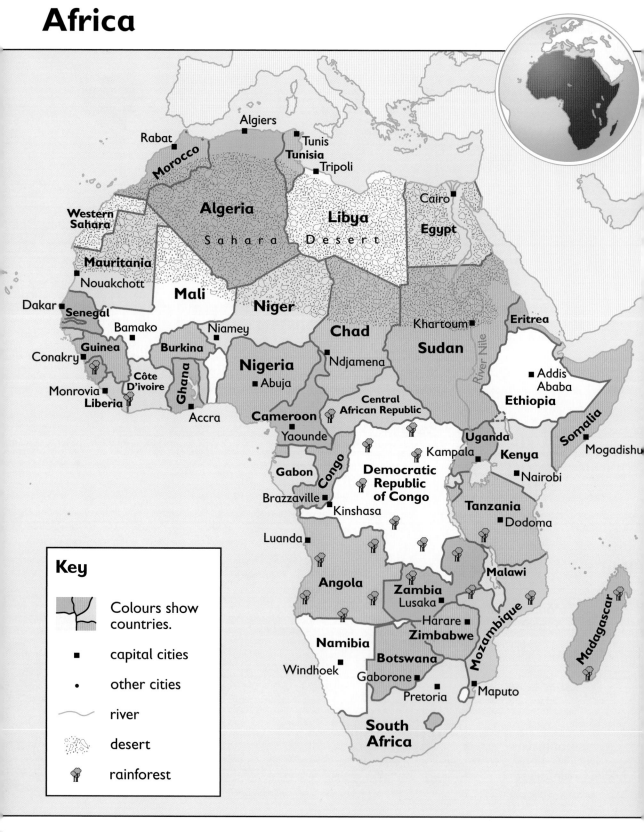

Key

Colours show countries.

■   capital cities

•   other cities

～   river

desert

rainforest

Africa is the hottest continent.

Oceania

Nauru

Papua
New Guinea

Solomon
Islands

Tuvalu

Port
Moresby

Vanuatu

Fiji

Great Sandy
Desert

New
Caledonia

A u s t r a l i a

Brisbane

Great Victoria
Desert

Perth

Adelaide

Sydney
Canberra

Melbourne

New
Zealand

Wellington

Australia has many
strange animals.

There are lots of islands in Oceania.

Antarctica

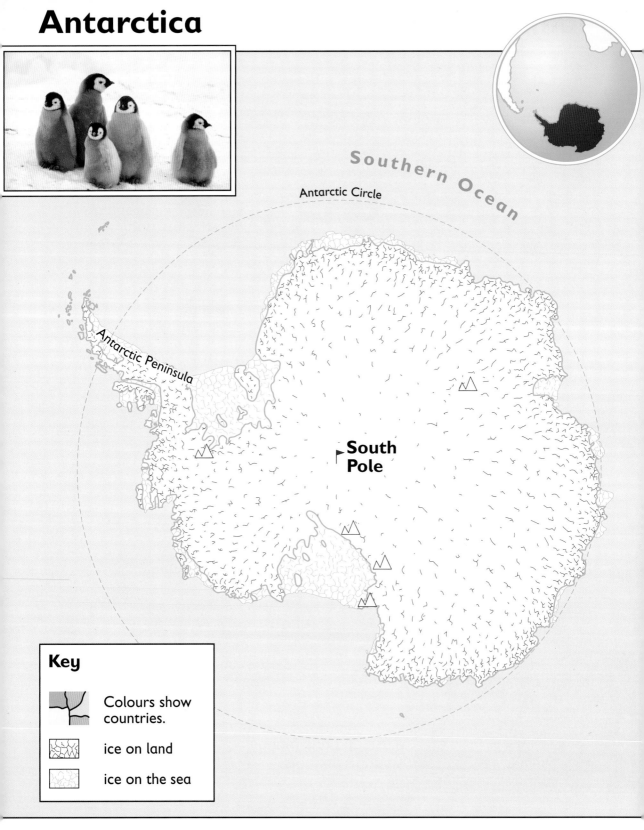

Southern Ocean

Antarctic Circle

Antarctic Peninsula

▶ South
Pole

Key

	Colours show countries.
	ice on land
	ice on the sea

Antarctica is land covered in ice.

The Arctic Ocean

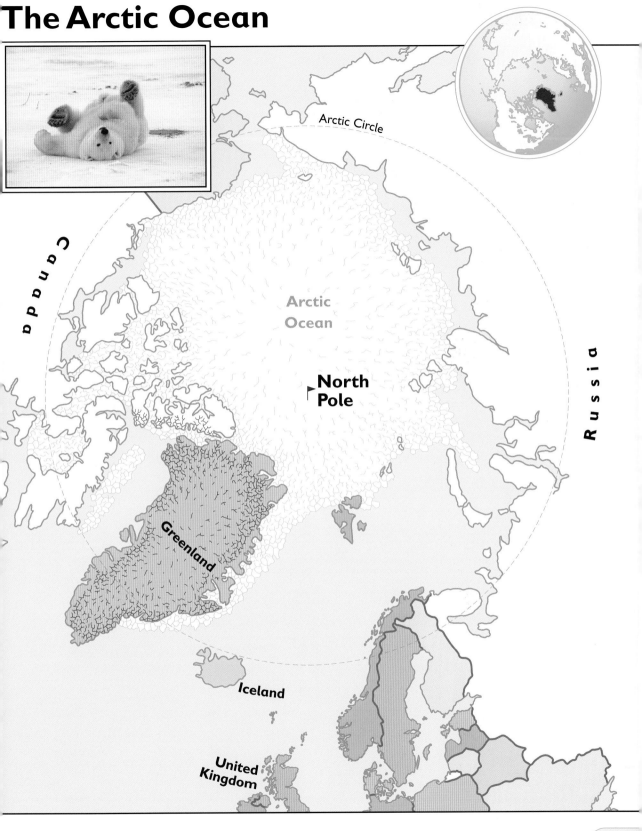

Canada

Arctic Circle

Arctic
Ocean

▶ North
Pole

Russia

Greenland

Iceland

United
Kingdom

The Arctic Ocean is frozen water.

This is Great Britain and Ireland from space

The British Isles

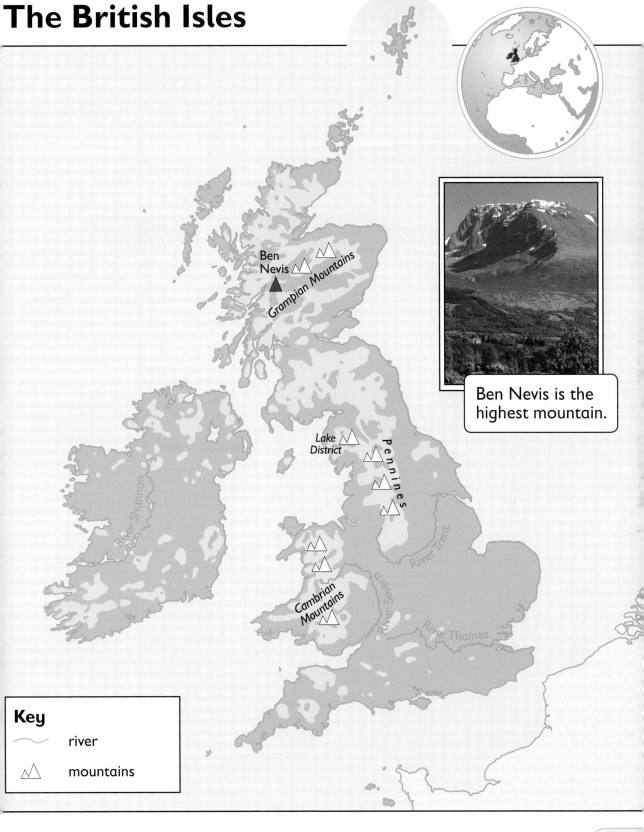

Ben Nevis is the highest mountain.

Key

~ river

⩕ mountains

This is a map of Great Britain and Ireland. 29

The British Isles

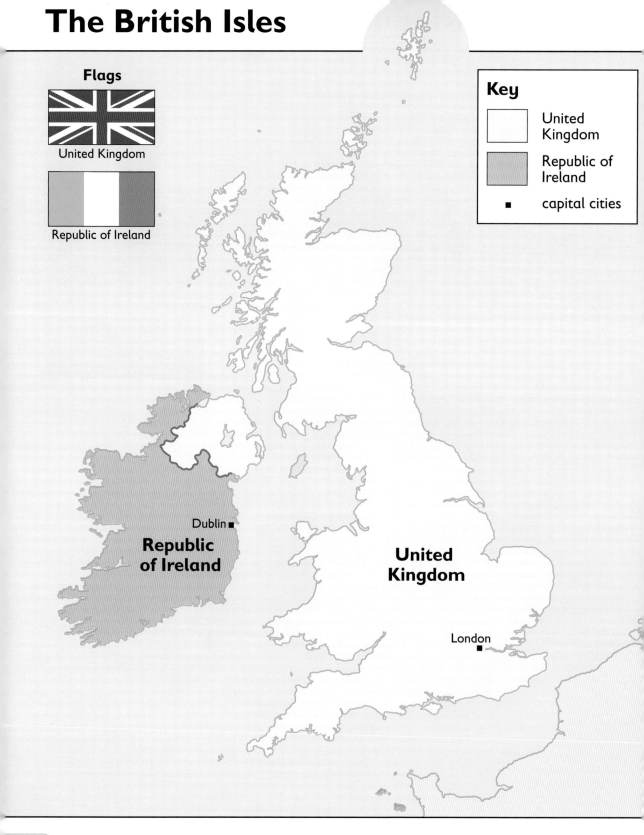

Flags

United Kingdom

Republic of Ireland

Key

United Kingdom

Republic of Ireland

■ capital cities

Dublin ■

Republic of Ireland

United Kingdom

London ■

There are two countries in the British Isles

The United Kingdom

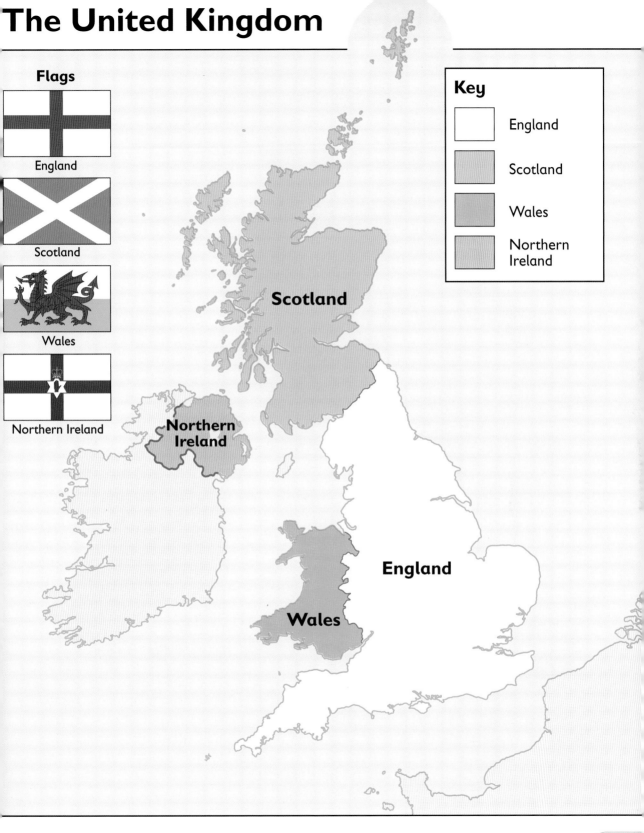

Flags

England

Scotland

Wales

Northern Ireland

Key

England

Scotland

Wales

Northern Ireland

Scotland

Northern Ireland

England

Wales

The United Kingdom has four parts.

The United Kingdom

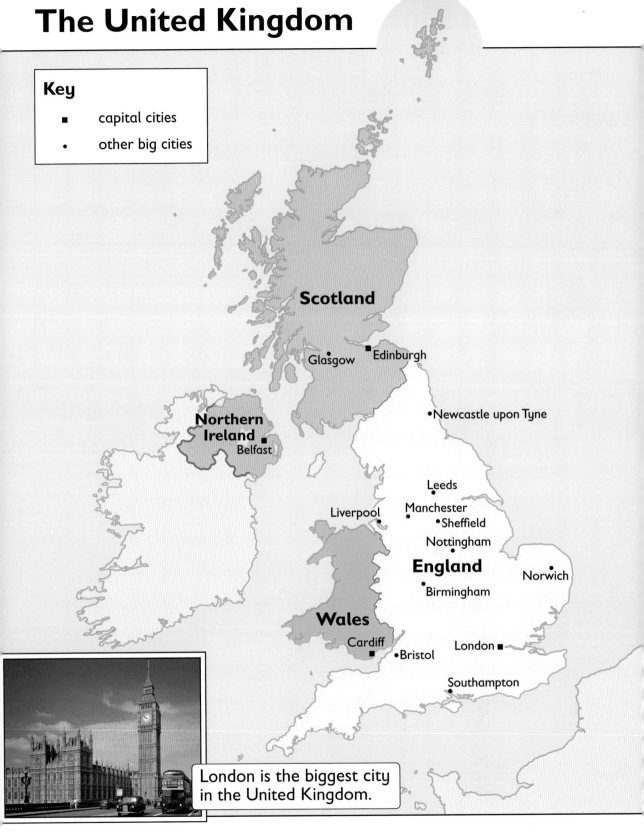

Key

■   capital cities

•   other big cities

Scotland

•Glasgow   ■ Edinburgh

Northern Ireland

■ Belfast

•Newcastle upon Tyne

•Leeds

Manchester
•   •Sheffield
•Liverpool

Nottingham
•

England

•Norwich

•Birmingham

Wales

Cardiff
■   •Bristol

London ■

•Southampton

London is the biggest city in the United Kingdom.

There are many big cities.

World Flags

 Afghanistan

 Albania

 Algeria

 Andorra

 Angola

 Argentina

 Armenia

 Australia

 Austria

 Azerbaijan

 Bahamas

 Bahrain

 Bangladesh

 Barbados

 Belarus

 Belgium

 Bolivia

 Bosnia-Herzegovina

 Botswana

 Brazil

 Bulgaria

 Burkina

 Burundi

 Cambodia

 Cameroon

 Canada

 Chad

 Chile

 China

 Colombia

 Congo

 Congo, Dem. Rep.

 Costa Rica

 Côte d'Ivoire

 Croatia

 Cuba

 Cyprus

 Czech Republic

 Denmark

 Dominica

 Dominican Republic

 Ecuador

 Egypt

 El Salvador

 Eritrea

 Estonia

 Ethiopia

 Fiji

 Finland

 France

 Gabon

 Gambia

Georgia

Germany

Ghana

Greece

Grenada

Guatemala

Guinea

Haiti

Honduras

Hungary

Iceland

India

Indonesia

Iran

Iraq

Ireland

Israel

Italy

Jamaica

Japan

Jordan

Kazakhstan

Kenya

Kuwait

Latvia

Lebanon